CW00403442

Spelling, Punctuation, and Grammar Practice

Includes Answer Key and a List of Irregular Verbs

Revised First Edition

Obinna C. Chukukere

First Edition published in 2019

This Revised First Edition published in February 2020
by English Pamphlets, an imprint of BINNACH BOOKS, Basildon, England

www.BINNACHBOOKS.com

ISBN: 9781691039852

To my wife, Ugochi
To my children: Chijioke, Chinenye, Chinemerem

CONTENTS

INTRODUCTION

Inspiration
The inspiration for this book came from my years of teaching English language in UK further education colleges and privately. It is a collection of the common errors made by my students in their grammar, spelling, and punctuation.

Layout of this book
The book is set out in a simple multiple-choice question format, comprising of 2-answer, 3-answer, and 4-answer options.

There are three sections, covering spellings, punctuation and grammar. For easy reference, question numbers are preceded by alphabets: **S** for spellings, **P** for punctuation and **G** for grammar.

All the answers (including tips and explanations) to all the questions, are given on the back pages.

Using this book
Use this book as you wish, to help you revise and reinforce your knowledge of your spellings and punctuation marks, word classes (parts of speech), and grammar, including sentences. It's best if you attempt the questions first and then look up the answers, tips and explanations in the answer sections.

1

CONFUSING SPELLINGS

This Unit focuses on some commonly confused spellings and words. Attempt the questions, then see the answers, explanations and tips on the back pages.

S1. Which of the spellings is correct for writing materials?
a) stationary
b) stationery
c) stationarey

S2. Which spelling is correct?
a) heigth
b) height
c) hieght

S3. Which spelling is correct?
a) grammar
b) grammer

S4. Which spelling is correct?
a) accomodate
b) accommodate

S5. Which spelling is correct?
a) embarras
b) embrass
c) embarrass
d) embarass

S6. Which spelling is correct?
a) cemetery
b) cemetry
c) cemetary

S7. Which spelling is correct?
a) millenium
b) milennium
c) millennium

S8. Which spelling is correct?
a) acheivement
b) acheivment
c) achievement
d) achievment

S9. Which spelling is correct?
a) decieve
b) deceive

S10. Which spelling is correct?
a) vein
b) vien

S11. Which spelling is correct?
a) sincerely
b) sincerelly
c) sincerly

S12. Which spelling is correct?
a) seperate
b) separate

S13. Which spelling is correct?
a) estacy
b) ecstasy
c) estasy
d) ecstacy

S14. Which spelling is correct?
a) commitment
b) commitement
c) committment
d) committement

S15. Which spelling is correct?
a) accummulate
b) accumulate
c) acummulate

S16. Which spelling is correct?
a) ommission
b) omision
c) omission

S17. Which spelling is correct?
a) disappoint
b) dissappoint
c) dissapoint

S18. Which spelling is correct?
a) decafeinated
b) decaffeinated
c) decaffienated
d) decaffinated

S19. Which spelling is correct?
a) flouride
b) flooride
c) floride
d) fluoride

S20. Which spelling is correct?
a) pasttime
b) passtime
c) pastime

S21. Which spelling is correct?
a) appearance
b) appearence

S22. Which spelling is correct?
a) arguement
b) argument

S23. Which spelling is correct?
a) bizzarre
b) bizzare
c) bizarre

S24. Which spelling is correct?
a) basically
b) basicaly
c) basicly

S25. Which spelling is correct?
a) calender
b) calendar

S26. Which spelling is correct?
a) definately
b) definitely
c) definitly

S27. Which spelling is correct?
a) seize
b) sieze

S28. Which spelling is correct?
a) Farenheit
b) Fahrenheit
c) Farhrenheit

S29. Which spelling is correct?
a) foreign
b) foriegn

S30. Which spelling is correct?
a) liase
b) laise
c) liaise

S31. Which spelling is correct?
a) occasion
b) occassion
c) ocassion

S32. Which spelling is correct?
a) receive
b) recieve

S33. Which spelling is correct?
a) wierd
b) weird

S34. Which spelling is correct?
a) thiner
b) thinner

S35. Which spelling is correct?
a) successfull
b) succesful
c) successful

S36. Which spelling is correct?
a) tatoo
b) tattoo

S37. Which spelling is correct?
a) tommorow
b) tommorrow
c) tomorow
d) tomorrow

S38. Which spelling is correct?
a) interupt
b) interrupt

S39. Which spelling is correct?
a) humorous
b) humourous

S40. Which spelling is correct?
a) irresistable
b) irresistible

S41. Which spelling refers to edible things?
a) desert
b) dessert

S42. Which spelling is correct?
a) misspelt (also *misspelled*)
b) mispelt (also *mispelled*)

2

PUNCTUATION

This Unit focuses on different types of punctuation marks, including inverted comma, hyphen, colon, semicolon, etc. Attempt the questions, then see the answers, explanations and tips on the back pages.

P1. Which sentence uses a question mark correctly?
a) "How much further do I have to cycle," moaned Sajid?
b) "How much further? do I have to cycle," moaned Sajid.
c) "How much further do I have to cycle?" moaned Sajid.

P2. *The dogs owner couldnt see the cat.* **What's missing in this sentence?**
a) question mark
b) apostrophe
c) speech marks

P3. A sentence can end with a question mark, a full stop, or an exclamation mark.
a) false
b) true

P4. Which sentence uses brackets correctly?
a) Ring me at home (you have my number) so we can chat.
b) Ring me at home you have my number (so we can chat).
c) Ring me (at home you have my number) so we can chat.
d) (Ring me) at home you have my number so we can chat.

P5. Which sentence uses a hyphen correctly?
a) We saw a man eating-shark at the aquarium.
b) We saw a man-eating-shark at the aquarium.
c) We saw a man-eating shark at the aquarium.
d) We saw a man eating shark at-the-aquarium.

P6. *Hearing a cat he jumped into the pond.* What's missing in this sentence?
a) comma
b) apostrophe
c) full stop

P7. Which sentence uses a semicolon correctly?
a) The wind was; very strong the kite flew high in the sky.

b) The wind was very strong; the kite flew high in the sky.

c) The wind was very strong, the kite; flew high in the sky.

d) The wind was very strong, the kite flew; high in the sky.

P8. You're all stars! The apostrophe in this sentence shows

a) omission/contraction.

b) possession.

P9. *Let's eat Michael.* Is anything wrong with this sentence?

a) No, nothing is wrong.

b) Yes, something is wrong.

P10. *The crowd listened to the womens stories.* Is anything wrong with this sentence?

a) No, the sentence is correct.

b) Yes, something is wrong.

P11. *My new college is called catwalk college.* Is this sentence correct?

a) Yes, the sentence is correct.

b) No, it's not correct.

P12. *Fiona Is going to The USA on Sunday.* Is anything wrong with this sentence?

a) No, there's nothing wrong.

b) Yes, something is wrong.

P13. *Sam's bike was lying on the ground.* **The apostrophe in this sentence shows**
a) possession.
b) omission/contraction.

P14. *My Friend pia travel to Italy yesterday.* **Is this sentence correct?**
a) Yes, the sentence is correct.
b) No, the sentence is wrong.

P15. Which sentence uses a colon correctly?
a) We had to buy the following: jam, butter, cream and scones.
b) We had to buy: the following jam, butter, cream and scones.
c) We had to buy the following jam: butter, cream and scones.
d) We had: to buy the following jam, butter, cream and scones.

P16. Which sentence uses a comma correctly?
a) Before, the end of the game the opposition left the pitch.
b) Before the end of the game, the opposition left the pitch.
c) Before the end of the game the opposition left, the pitch.

P17. *We packed the following swimsuits, hats, beach towels and sun cream.* **This sentence needs a**
a) semicolon.

b) colon.

c) question mark.

d) exclamation mark.

P18. Which sentence uses a colon correctly?

a) We've chosen two cities to visit London: and Paris.

b) We've chosen two cities to visit: London and Paris.

c) We've chosen two cities: to visit London and Paris.

P19. Which sentence uses a semicolon correctly?

a) The weather; in June was warm it was a sunny month.

b) The weather in June; was warm it was a sunny month.

c) The weather in June was warm; it was a sunny month.

P20. Which sentence uses speech marks correctly?

a) "Tickets please!" shouted the driver. "All tickets, please!"

b) "Tickets please! shouted the driver." "All tickets, please!"

P21. Which sentence uses an apostrophe to show omission/contraction?

a) The waiter took the customer's order.

b) We won't be able to see from here.

P22. Which sentence uses an apostrophe to show possession/ownership?
a) This is my house; the next one is James'.
b) Jane didn't find her keys.

P23. Which sentence is punctuated correctly?
a) I have three hobbies; painting, reading and hockey.
b) I have three hobbies: painting, reading and hockey.
c) I have three hobbies painting reading and hockey.

P24. Which sentence uses a comma correctly?
a) Although, she left on time, she was late for school.
b) Although she left on time, she was late for school.
c) Although she left, on time she was late for school.

P25. In a restaurant, the waiter is serving many customers. Which sentence below is correctly punctuated?
a) The waiter took the customers order's.
b) The waiter took the customer's orders.
c) The waiter took the customers' orders.

P26. *The teacher asked, "Are your exams starting next Monday"?* Does this sentence use inverted commas correctly?
a) Yes
b) No

3

GRAMMAR

This Unit focuses on grammar, including word classes, and sentences. Attempt the questions, then see the answers, explanations and tips on the back pages.

G1. What is the word class of each word in bold letters? The excited child **talked loudly**.
a) talked (adverb) / loudly (adjective)
b) talked (adjective) / loudly (adverb)
c) talked (verb) / loudly (adverb)
d) talked (adverb) / loudly (verb)

G2. I reluctantly went on holiday to sunny Spain. The **adverb** in this sentence is
a) reluctantly.
b) Spain.
c) went.
d) sunny.

G3. *I asked Joe: How come your working every day of the week?* Is this sentence wrong or correct?
a) The sentence is correct.
b) The sentence is wrong.

G4. Which sentence is **correct**?
a) I hanged the picture yesterday.
b) I hung the picture yesterday.

G5. Which sentence contains two **verbs**?
a) Sam hugged his poorly sister gently.
b) The child jumped and screamed in anger.
c) The computer whirred noisily on the desk.
d) Mike skipped joyfully to school.

G6. The **comparative** form of bad is...
a) good.
b) worst.
c) worse.

G7. The **superlative** form of lovely is...
a) lovelier.
b) more lovely.
c) not lovely.
d) loveliest.

G8. The **comparative** form of good is...
a) best.
b) better.
c) well.

G9. *The loudest kid was obviously shouting!* The **adjective** in this sentence is...
a) kid.
b) obviously.
c) loudest.
d) shouting.

G10. Identify a **noun** and a **verb** in this sentence: *You cycled to work last week.*
a) verb: *you* / noun: *cycled*
b) verb: *work* / noun: *work*
c) verb: *cycled* / noun: *work*
d) verb: *last* / noun: *to*

G11. *Their are twenty teachers in this college.* Is this sentence wrong or correct?
a) It's correct.
b) It's wrong.

G12. The **plural** form of belief is...
a) beliefs.
b) believes.

G13. What is the word class of each word in bold letters? The **excited child** talked loudly.
a) excited: *verb* / child: *noun*
b) excited: *noun* / child: *verb*
c) excited: *noun* / child: *adjective*
d) excited: *adjective* / child: *noun*

G14. Complete the sentence with **I** or **me:** *My teacher gave Ryan and.........extra homework.*
a) me
b) I

G15. *The bear was hiding in the cave.* The **preposition** in this sentence is...
a) bear.
b) cave.
c) in.
d) hiding.

G16. *My favourite pastimes are cooking my pets and painting.*
a) This sentence is correct.
b) This sentence is incorrect.

G17. *The children had to trudge through the mud.* The **preposition** in this sentence is...
a) mud.
b) trudge.
c) the.
d) through.

G18. *The loudest lion was obviously the smallest!* The **verb** in this sentence is...
a) loudest.
b) was.
c) lion.
d) smallest.

G19. Tick any **correct** sentence.
a) the chef loves cooking.
b) The chef loves cooking
c) The chef loves cooking.
d) The chef love cooking.

G20. *My granny has many sheeps.* Is this sentence correct?
a) No, it's not correct.
b) Yes, it's correct.

G21. Choose the words that are **antonyms** of bright.
a) dark / dreary
b) radiant / polished
c) blazing / brilliant
d) vivid / twinkling

G22. Add a **conjunction** to this sentence: *I like horse-riding...........it is exciting.*
a) because
b) and
c) but
d) so

G23. *Mikelle skipped joyfully to school.* The **adverb** in this sentence is...
a) Mikelle.
b) skipped.
c) school.
d) joyfully.

G24. Add a **conjunction** to this sentence: *Mrs. James is my teacher.........she makes learning fun.*
a) but
b) and
c) so
d) or

G25. Which of these sentences is **correct**?
a) I think its going to rain.
b) I think its' going to rain.
c) I think it's going to rain.

G26. *I happily ran through the scary forest.* In this sentence, **scary** is...
a) an adjective.
b) a verb.
c) an adverb.
d) a noun.

G27. Which sentence is **correct**?
a) You and me are friends.
b) You and I are friends.
c) I and you are friends.

G28. *I drove to my friend's house and we both went to Catwalk Cafe in his car.*
a) The proper noun in this sentence is car
b) The proper noun in this sentence is house.
c). The proper noun in this sentence is Catwalk Cafe.

G29. *I happily ran through the scary forest.* In this sentence, **happily** is...
a) an adjective.
b) an adverb.
c) a verb.
d) a noun.

G30. Choose **two** correct sentences.
a) I don't want no help.
b) I don't want any help.
c) I do not want any help.

G31. Sharon said: *'We are proud of **our school**.'* In the sentence, which pronoun can replace **our school**?
a) ours
b) it

G32. *I reluctantly went on holiday to sunny Spain.* The **adjective** in this sentence is...
a) holiday.
b) sunny.
c) Spain.
d) reluctantly.

G33. Which sentence uses **brackets** correctly?
a) Nathaniel (my best friend) came to my house yesterday.
b) Nathaniel (my best friend came to my house) yesterday.
c) (Nathaniel my best friend) came to my house yesterday.

G34. *Yesterday, the newspaper wasn't printed!* The **noun** in this sentence is...
a) yesterday.
b) printed.
c) newspaper.
d) wasn't.

G35. Choose two **correct** sentences.
a) The box are ready.
b) The box of sweets are ready.
c) The box is ready.
d) The box of sweets is ready.

G36. *The loudest kid was obviously shouting!* The **adverb** in this sentence is...
a) loudest.
b) kid.
c) obviously.

G37. *The children went on a visit yesterday and bought souvenirs.* The **verbs** in this sentence are...
a) bought / visit.
b) went / visit.
c) went / bought.

G38. Which words are the **antonyms** of tough?
a) fragile / delicate
b) rough / hard
c) strong / hard
d) mean / aggressive

G39. *The dog chased...... down the road. ...... ran because we were scared.* Complete the gaps with the most appropriate **pronouns.**
a) I / She
b) her / He
c) us / We
d) them / They

G40. Complete the following sentence using either **I** or **me**. *The dog barked at Joe and...*
a) I.
b) me.

G41. Complete the following sentence using either **I** or **me**. *Fred and......played a board game.*
a) me
b) I

G42. Which sentence is **correct**?
a) It was a late night for you and I.
b) It was a late night for you and me.

G43. Which is the **correct form** of these noun/verb pairs?
a) noun: prophecy / verb: prophesy
b) noun: prophesy / verb: prophecy

G44. Which is **correct** from these noun/verb pairs?
a) noun: advice / verb: advise
b) noun: advise / verb: advice

G45. Which is **correct** from these noun/verb pairs?
a) noun: device / verb: devise
b) noun: devise / verb: device

G46. Which is **correct** from these noun/verb pairs?
a) noun: practise / verb: practice
b) noun: practice / verb: practise

G47. *The sun shone through the trees onto the car.*
The **nouns** in the sentence are...
a) shone / trees / the.
b) through / car / onto.
c) sun / trees / car.
d) trees / car / through.

G48. *The hurdler jumped over the hurdles.* The **preposition** in this sentence is...
a) over.
b) hurdler.
c) jumped.
d) hurdle.

G49. I **helped** the chatty little girl to play on the swing. The word in bold letters is...
a) a verb.
b) an adverb.
c) a noun.
d) an adjective.

G50. Choose the **wrong** sentence.
a) Was you at the party?
b) Were you at the party?

G51. I helped the **chatty** girl to play on the swing.
The word in bold letters is...
a) a verb.
b) a noun.
c) an adjective.
d) an adverb.

G52. I helped the chatty girl to **play** on the swing.
The word in bold letters is...
a) an adverb.
b) an adjective.
c) a noun.
d) a verb.

G53. The **plural** form of *leaf* is...
a) leafs.
b) leafes.
c) leaves.
d) leavs.

G54. I helped the chatty girl to play on the **swing**.
The word in bold letters is...
a) a noun.
b) an adverb.
c) an adjective.
d) a verb.

G55. Complete this sentence: *This is their house; it is...*
a) their's.
b) theirs.
c) theres.
d) thiers.

G56. The **plural** form of knife is...
a) knifes.
b) knives.
c) knifves.

G57. Which sentence contains two **verbs**?
a) Samuel packed his bag and ran to school.
b) Tiegan ran happily and joyously to school.
c) Jasmin packed her bag with toys and games.
d) The phone rang in the hallway.

G58. *The mouse scuttled quickly and silently across the floor.* The **adverbs** in this sentence are...
a) mouse / scuttled.
b) across / the.
c) quickly / silently.
d) scuttled / floor.

G59. Which is correct from these noun/verb pairs?
a) noun: alter / verb: altar
b) noun: altar / verb: alter

G60. Complete this sentence: *That car belongs to Sandra; It's...*

a) her's.
b) hers.
c) hers'.
d) hers's.

G61. *After my friend left, I started doing my homework at 2 o'clock.* This is an example of a...
a) topic sentence.
b) complex sentence.
c) simple sentence.
d) compound sentence.

G62. *This is my instruments.* Is this sentence correct?
a) The sentence is incorrect.
b) The sentence is correct.

G63. *I woke up at 10 am yesterday and i had a big breakfast.* Is anything wrong with this sentence?
a) Yes, something is wrong.
b) No, nothing is wrong.

G64. *Despite the bad weather, the fair raised a lot of money for the charity.* This sentence is a...
a) topic sentence.
b) simple sentence.
c) complex sentence.
d) compound sentence.

G65. *Everybody in the college are finishing today.* Is this sentence correct?
a) Yes

b) No

G66. *The library assistant told Joe to return the* **book** *he borrowed.* In this sentence, the word in bold letters is...
a) a noun.
b) a verb.
c) an adverb.
d) an adjective.

G67. *John told the hotel manager to* **book** *two rooms for his guests.* In this sentence, the word in bold letters is a...
a) noun.
b) verb.
c) adverb.
d) adjective.

G68. Choose the words that are **antonyms** of beautiful.
a) unattractive / unsightly
b) plentiful / bountiful
c) pretty / lovely
d) difficult / hard

G69. *Everything have been done.* Is this sentence correct?
a) Yes
b) No

G70. Here are three sentences. Which is **wrong**?

a) Paul didn't want any more food.
b) Paul didn't want more food.
c) Paul didn't want no more food.

G71. *After the race had finished, the two drivers shook hands.* The **main clause** in this sentence is...
a) *the two drivers shook hands.*
b) *After the race had finished.*

G72. *Although they were tired, the children kept running.* The **minor clause** in this sentence is...
a) *Although they were tired.*
b) *the children kept running.*

G73. *I'll go swimming tomorrow.* The **adverb** in this sentence is...
a) swimming.
b) tomorrow.
c) go.

G74. Choose a tag question to complete this sentence. *They've been here before, ...*
a) have they?
b) haven't they?

G75. *On Thursday, Millie played at her friend's house.* The **subject** in this sentence is...
a) Thursday.
b) Millie.
c) house.
d) played.

G76. *Maggie stroked the cat.* The **object** in this sentence is...
a) stroked.
b) the.
c) cat.
d) carefully.

G77. Which sentence uses **plural noun** correctly?
a) My favourite superheroes are Batman and Superman.
b) The thiefs stole my purse.
c) The bush in the school yard is full of berrys.
d) Remi and Regi were the twin boy's.

G78. *The Alsatian came out last night and its barking filled the air.* This sentence is a...
a) simple sentence.
b) compound sentence.
c) complex sentence.

G79. Choose a tag question to complete this sentence:
You don't think Andrea went to the cinema yesterday,
...
a) don't you?
b) did you?
c) do you?
d) didn't you?

G80. Choose a tag question to complete this sentence: *We haven't finished, ...*
a) haven't we?
b) have we?
c) we haven't?

G81. A **definite article** is used to refer to a specific thing or person. An **indefinite article** is used to refer to a person or thing in a non-specific way.
a) false
b) true

G82. *The* is a definite article; *a, an* are indefinite articles.
a) true
b) false

▪ ANSWERS
▪ TIPS
▪ EXPLANATIONS

Answers to Unit 1

Confusing Spellings

S1. Option B [stationery] (spelt with *e*) is correct

Stationery is a noun, referring to items of writing, for example pens, papers, envelopes, and pencils. The other *stationary* (spelt with *a*) is an adjective, referring to something that is not moving or not changing.

S2. Option B [height] is correct

This word is a noun. It refers to how high something is; the distance between the top and the base of an object, or structure, or from head to foot (for human beings).

S3. Option A [grammar] is correct

Grammar is a noun. It refers to how we use different words in different situations and for different uses, and how we combine these words to make sentences.

S4. Option B [accommodate] is correct

This word is a verb, meaning to provide a place for someone to live or to store something or to make space for somebody/something.

Tip: Remember that the spelling has double 'cc' and double 'mm'.

S5. Option C [embarrass] is correct

This word is a verb. It means to make someone feel ashamed or to feel awkward.

Tip: Remember that the word has double 'rr' and double 'ss'.

S6. Option A [cemetery] is correct

Cemetery is a noun which means a place (an area of ground) where dead people are buried.

Tip: There isn't any 'a' in the spelling of *cemetery*.

S7. Option C [millennium] is correct

This word, also a noun, refers to a period of 1000 years. The plural forms are *millennia* or *milleniums*.

Tip: Remember, the spelling has double 'll' and

double '*nn*' in the singular and in the plural forms.

S8. Option C [achievement] is correct

Another noun, *achievement* means succeeding at doing something or reaching an aim.
Tip: The verb form of *achievement* is to *achieve*.

S9. Option B [deceive] is correct

This word is a verb. It means to make someone to believe, or to accept that something that is false, is true.
Tip: Remember that in *deceive, receipt,* and *receive,* the '*e*' comes before the '*i*'.

S10. Option A [vein] is correct

This word is a noun referring to the tubes that carry blood around the body, passing through the heart.

S11. Option A [sincerely] is correct

This word is an adverb. It conveys a sense of honesty. It comes from *sincere* which is an adjective.

Tip: The word *sincerely* is usually used in the closing greeting of formal letters, like this: *Yours sincerely* (when you have the addressee's name). But if the formal letter begins with *Dear Sir* or *Dear Madam*, the closing greeting should be *Yours faithfully*.

S12. Option B [separate] is correct

This word is a verb as well as an adjective. As an adjective, it means something that is independent, not joined to anything, not shared. As a verb, it means to split or to divide into parts.

S13. Option B [ecstasy] is correct

This word is a noun which means a feeling of great or extreme happiness or delight.

S14. Option A [commitment] is correct

This word, a noun, refers to a person's willingness to do something, a firm decision to do something. **Tip:** Remember that although *commitment* has one 't', *committed* has double 'tt'.

S15. Option B [accumulate] is correct

This word is a verb which means to pile up or to collect a large quantity of things over a long period of time.

S16. Option C [omission] is correct

This is a noun. It refers to a situation when something or someone is not included in something.

S17. Option A [disappoint] is correct

This word is a verb. It refers to a situation when someone fails to make the hopes or wishes of another to come true. It also means to make someone unhappy.

Tip: The verb is *disappoint*, the noun is *disappointment*.

S18. Option B [decaffeinated] is correct

This word is an adjective. It describes coffee (or tea) that has the caffeine removed.

S19. Option D [fluoride] is correct

This word is a noun. It is the name of a chemical in toothpaste, which helps to prevent tooth decay.

Tip: In some areas of the UK, fluoride is sometimes added to the water supply. This is called *fluoridation*.

S20. Option C [pastime] is correct

This word is a noun. It means an enjoyable thing we do.

Tip: Your pastime could be a hobby or a game, or even a DIY (do it yourself) activity.

S21. Option A [appearance] is correct

This is another noun. It can have several meanings: being in the present, the way someone or something looks, being present for a short period of time.

S22. Option B [argument] is correct

This word is a noun. It means a disagreement, a quarrel, or a process of disagreeing. It also means a reason (or reasons) why you support or oppose something.

Tip: The verb *argue* has an 'e' in the spelling, but the 'e' isn't there in *argument*.

S23. Option C [bizarre] is correct

An adjective, *bizarre* describes something that is odd, strange, or unusual.
Tip: To form the adverb, we add *'ly'*: *bizarrely*.

S24. Option A [basically] is correct

This word is an adverb. It is used when we refer to something at the simplest form or the most important feature of something.

S25. Option B [calendar] is correct

The word calendar is a noun. It is a printed table or chart that shows all the days, weeks, and months of the year. Organisations (like schools) also have calendars which show dates and events that are important to them.

S26. Option B [definitely] is correct

You can tell by the *'ly'* that this word is an adverb. It means without any doubt.

S27. Option A [seize] is correct

This word is a verb, meaning to take hold of something quickly, to take possession of, or keep something by force.

S28. Option B [Fahrenheit] is correct

This word is an adjective. It is also a noun. It is a scale or unit of temperature at which water freezes at 32 degrees and boils at 212 degrees.
Tip: Fahrenheit is actually the name of a German scientist who invented the mercury thermometer. Weather temperature can be measured in Fahrenheit, to show how warm or how cold.

S29. Option A [foreign] is correct

Foreign is an adjective. It describes something that does not belong naturally to a place or to someone; or something that is not known to someone.

S30. Option C [liaise] is correct

Liaise is a verb. It means to exchange information or to engage with someone or with an organization towards achieving an outcome.

S31. Option A [occasion] is correct

This word can be a verb and a noun. As a noun, it means a special event, or a period of time when something or an event happens. As a verb, *occasion* is used in formal situations to show a cause.

S32. Option A [receive] is correct

This word is a verb. It means to get or be given something. In a formal sense, it means to welcome a visitor or a guest.
Tip: Keep in mind that in *deceive, receipt,* and *receive,* the '*e*' comes before the '*i*'.

S33. Option B [weird] is correct

Weird is an adjective. It describes something that is very strange and unusual, or something that is unexpected, or not natural.
Tip: Remind yourself that in the spelling, the '*e*' comes before the '*i*'.

S34. Option B [thinner] is correct

This word is a comparative adjective. It comes from the adjective *thin*. It describes something or someone that is not fat, or not thick. It is used to compare how slim or how fat someone or something is.

Tip: Remember that although the adjective *thinner* is spelt with '*nn*', the adverb *thinly* is spelt with one '*n*'.

S35. Option C [successful] is correct

This is an adjective. It describes a wanted achievement, or an achievement that is hoped for.

Tip: Don't forget that although the adjective *successful* is spelt with one '*l*', the adverb *successfully* is spelt with '*ll*'. Note that both spellings have '*cc*' and '*ss*'.

S36. Option B [tattoo] is correct

This word is a noun and a verb. As a verb, it means to mark a person's skin with a word, image, or pattern.

As a noun, it refers to any decoration, image, word, or pattern on a person's skin.

S37. Option D [tomorrow] is correct

This word is a noun. It can also be used as an adverb. As an adverb, it shows when an action or an event happens. As a noun, it is the day after today.

Tip: Keep in mind that the spelling has one 'm' and spelt with 'rr'.

S38. Option B [interrupt] is correct

This word is a verb. It means to prevent something from happening, or to break the sequence or flow of something. It also means to stop someone from speaking for a short period of time.

Tip: Remember the 'rr' in the spelling.

S39. Option A [humorous] is correct

The word *humorous* is an adjective. It describes something that is funny or amusing.

S40. Option B [irresistible] is correct

This word is an adjective. It describes something (or someone) that is pleasant and too good to be refused, or too good to be rejected, or too good to be avoided.

S41. Option B [dessert] is correct

This word is a noun. It refers to a sweet food or fruit that is eaten at the end of a meal, or as part of a three-course meal.

Tip: The word *dessert* (spelt with 'ss') is different from *desert* (spelt with one 's').

Desert is both a noun and a verb. As a noun, (with the pronunciation *dez-ert*), it means a wide area of dry and dusty sand.
As a verb, (with the pronunciation *diz-ert*), it means to escape, to run away or to leave someone or something.

S42. Option A [misspelt] (also misspelled) is correct

This word is a verb. It means to wrongly spell a word. **Tip:** Both *misspelt* and *misspelled* are correct spellings.

Answers to Unit **2**

Punctuation

P1: Correct answer is option C ["How much further do I have to cycle?" moaned Sajid.]

Keep in mind that when the quoted direct speech is a question, then the question mark should be within the quotation marks.

Tip: Quotation marks are also known as *inverted commas* or *speech marks*.
Remember that inverted commas can either be single ('…') or double ("…") but not to be mixed and matched.

P2: Correct answer is option B, [apostrophe]

Let's look at the sentence again. *The dogs owner couldnt see the cat.* This sentence needs an apostrophe before the 's' in *dogs* (that is *dog's*, if it's just one dog), or after the 's' if there are more than one dog (that is *dogs'*). Then there should be another apostrophe before the 't' in *couldnt*, so it

---

becomes *couldn't*, which is a contraction (a short form) of *could not*.

Get it right: An apostrophe is used to show possession (that something belongs to someone or to another thing). Example: *Ian's cats.*

Apostrophe is also used to show omission, particularly in contractions, to indicate a missing letter or letters. For example: *you are – you're, could not – couldn't.*

P3: Correct answer is option B [true]

Yes, a sentence can end with either a question mark *(?)*, a full stop *(.)* or an exclamation mark *(!)*.

We use a question mark to end a sentence that asks a question.
We use an exclamation mark to end a sentence that shows strong emotion.
We use a full stop to mark the end of a complete sentence.
A full stop is also called a *period* in American English.

P4: Correct answer is option A [Ring me at home (you have my number) so we can chat.]

Usually we use brackets to insert extra information (or word or phrase) within a sentence. We always use them in pairs around the extra information.

Tip: Brackets are also called *parentheses*, particularly in American English.

P5: Correct answer is option C [We saw a man-eating shark at the aquarium.]

A hyphen (-) is used to connect two words so that the two words become one, in order to convey a particular meaning.

Get it right: In the sentences below, notice the difference in meaning between the use of a hyphen (in sentence 1) and without a hyphen (in sentence 2).
1. A cross-section of the community attended the meeting.
2. A cross section of the community attended the meeting.

In sentence 1, *cross-section of the community* means a sample part of the community.

In sentence 2, *cross section of the community* means an angry group of the community.

P6: Correct answer is option A [comma]

To fully convey the meaning in the sentence, you need a comma after *cat*, to indicate a pause after the first clause. So, the correct sentence looks like this: *Hearing a cat, he jumped into the pond.*

Tip: The main functions of a comma are to clarify information, to separate items in a list, to mark a pause in the sentence, or to separate clauses. Commas are also used before and after someone's name who has been mentioned before or is being described.

P7: Correct answer is option B [The wind was very strong; the kite flew high in the sky.]

The main function of a semicolon is to separate two or more related independent clauses within a sentence; each clause should be able to stand as a complete sentence. The sentence in answer *P7* above is a good example.

Tip: Try not to use a semicolon to connect a main clause with a minor clause.

P8: Correct answer is option A [omission / contraction]

The use of an apostrophe in this question shows an omission or a contraction.

Get it right: An apostrophe is used in contractions to indicate a missing letter or letters. For example: *you are – you're, could not – couldn't.*

An apostrophe is used to show possession/ownership (that something belongs to someone or to another thing). For example: *Ian's cats.*

P9: Correct answer is option B [Yes, something is wrong.]

Let's eat Michael. To fully convey the meaning in this sentence, you need a comma after *eat,* to indicate a pause after the first clause. If not, then you might as well go on and eat Michael.

So, the correct sentence should look like this: *Let's eat, Michael.*

Tip: The main functions of a comma are: to clarify information, to separate items in a list, to mark a pause in the sentence, or to separate clauses. Commas are also used before and after someone's name who has been mentioned before or is being described.

P10: Correct answer is option B [Yes, something is wrong.]

Remember that an apostrophe is used to show possession/ownership (that something belongs to someone or to another thing). For example: *Ian's cats.*

Apostrophe is also used to show omission, particularly in contractions, to show that letters are missing. For example: *you are – you're, could not – couldn't.*

Get it right: Let's examine that sentence again. *The crowd listened to the womens stories.* Even though *women* is plural, it still needs an apostrophe before the *s*; this is to show that the stories are about the women – the stories belong to them. So, the correct sentence is *The crowd listened to the women's stories.*

P11: Correct answer is option B [No, it's not correct.]

Let's bring up the sentence again: *My new college is called catwalk college.* Although *catwalk* is just a noun, the *c* in catwalk (in the sentence) should be a capital letter because it is a proper noun in the sentence – it is a specific name. The *c* in *college* should also be a capital letter, if *college* is part of the name.

So, the correct sentence should look like this: *My new college is called Catwalk College.*

P12: Correct answer is B [Yes, something is wrong.]

In the sentence, (*Fiona Is going to The USA on Sunday.*), there is no need for the *i* in *Is* to be in capital letter. Also, there is no need for the *t* in *The USA* to be a capital letter. The *t* can only be in capital if *The* is part of the name *USA*.

So, the correct sentence should look like this: *Fiona is going to the USA on Sunday.*

P13: Correct answer is option A [possession]

The use of an apostrophe in this question indicates possession/ownership. Here is that sentence again: *Sam's bike was lying on the ground.* The apostrophe before the *s* shows that the bike belongs to Sam.

An apostrophe is used to show possession/ownership (that something belongs to someone or to another thing).

Apostrophe is also used to show omission, particularly in contractions, to indicate a missing letter or letters. For example: *could not – couldn't, do not – don't.*

P14: Correct answer is option B [No, the sentence is wrong.]

In the sentence, (*My Friend pia travel to Italy yesterday.*), there is no need for the capital *F* in *Friend*, as this is not a proper noun in the sentence.

The '*p*' in *pia* should be a capital letter because it is someone's name – a proper noun.

The verb *travel* should also be in the past simple tense, which is *travelled*, because Pia's trip to Italy happened *yesterday*.

So, the correct sentence looks like this: *My friend, Pia, travelled to Italy yesterday.*

Remember that a proper noun is the name of a specific thing, organization, person, place, or company. Proper nouns are spelt with an initial capital letter. Examples of the most common proper nouns are days of the week, festivals, titles, months of the year, your name, names of countries, etc.

P15: Correct answer is option A [We had to buy the following: jam, butter, cream and scones.]

A colon is used to explain, to add to, or to expand on what has been said before.

We can use a colon to link two clauses in a sentence, where the second clause usually explains the first. A colon can also introduce a list, as in the sentence in *P15* above.

P16: Correct answer is option B [Before the end of the game, the opposition left the pitch.]

This is a good example of the use of a comma, where it separates a minor clause from a main clause in a sentence.

Tips: The main functions of a comma are to clarify information, to separate items in a list, to mark a pause in the sentence, or to separate clauses.

Commas are also used before and after someone's name who has been mentioned before or is being described.

P17: Correct answer is option B [colon]

A colon is used to explain, to add to, or to expand on what has been said before.

We can use a colon to link two clauses in a sentence. The second clause usually explains the first.

A colon can also introduce a list, as in *What would you like on your sandwich: butter, jam, or marmalade?*

P18: Correct answer is option B [We've chosen two cities to visit: London and Paris.]

A colon is used to explain, to add to, or to expand on what has been said before.

We can use a colon to link two clauses in a sentence. The second clause usually explains the first. A colon can also introduce a list, as in the sentence in
P18 above.

P19: Correct answer is option C [The weather in June was warm; it was a sunny month.]

The main function of a semicolon is to separate two or more related independent clauses within a sentence; each clause should be able to stand as a complete sentence.

The sentence in answer *P19* above is a good example. Notice that **The weather in June was warm** is a complete sentence and *It was a sunny month* can also stand on its own.

Tip: Try not to use a semicolon to connect a main clause with a minor clause.

P20: Correct answer is option A ["Tickets please!" shouted the driver. "All tickets, please!"]

Notice that the exclamation mark is placed inside the speech marks because we are directly quoting the speaker - the driver.

Tip: Speech marks are also known as *quotation marks* or *inverted commas*. Remember that inverted commas can either be single ('...') or double ("...") but not to be mixed and matched.

P21: Correct answer is option B [We won't be able to see from here.]

The use of an apostrophe in this question

indicates an omission – a missing letter.

Apostrophe is used to show omission, particularly in contractions, to indicate a missing letter or letters. For example: *will not – won't, you are – you're.*

An apostrophe is also used to show possession/ownership (that something belongs to someone or to another thing). For example: *Ian's cats.*

P22: Correct answer is option A [This is my house; the next one is James'.]

The use of an apostrophe in this question indicates possession/ownership. The apostrophe after the *s* shows that the house belongs to James.

The apostrophe is placed after the *s* because *James* is someone's name. In this case, a second *s* is not usually needed for such names or words that end with *s*.

An apostrophe is used to show possession/ownership (that something belongs to someone or to another thing).

Apostrophe is also used to show omission, particularly in contractions, to indicate a missing letter or letters. For example: *could not – couldn't, will not – won't.*

P23: Correct answer is option B [I have three hobbies: painting, reading and hockey.]

A colon is used to explain, to add to, or to expand on what has been said before. We can use a colon to link two clauses in a sentence. The second clause usually explains the first.

A colon can also introduce a list, as in the sentence in *P23* above.

P24: Correct answer is option B, [Although she left on time, she was late for school.]

The comma is correctly used here because it separates the main clause from the minor clause in the sentence.

Tip: The main functions of a comma are to clarify information, to separate items in a list, to mark a pause in the sentence, or to separate clauses. Commas are also used before and after someone's name who has been mentioned before or is being described.

P25: Correct answer is option C [The waiter took

the customers' orders.]

The apostrophe is placed after the *s* because *customers* is plural – more than one. A second *s* is not usually needed for such plural words.

An apostrophe is used to show possession/ownership (that something belongs to someone or to another thing).

For example: *Sam's bike.* The apostrophe before the *s* shows possession/ownership, that the bike belongs to Sam.

Apostrophe is also used to show omission, particularly in contractions, to indicate a missing letter or letters. For example: *could not – couldn't, you are – you're.*

P26: Correct answer is B [No]

The question mark should be placed inside the inverted commas because it is part of the speech - in this case, a question.

So, the correct sentence should look like this: *The teacher asked, "Are your exams starting next Monday?"*

Tip: Inverted commas are also known as *quotation marks* or *speech marks.*

Remember that inverted commas can either be single ('...') or double ("...") but not to be mixed and matched.

Answers to Unit 3

Grammar

G1: Option C, [talked (verb) / loudly (adverb)]

Remember that a verb can be a visible or an invisible action, as well as a state of being. In the sentence, *talked*, a visible action, is the verb.

Adverb on the other hand, tells us *when*, *how*, or *where* the verb happens.

In the sentence (The excited child **talked loudly.**), *loudly* is the adverb. It gives more information on the *how* of the verb *talked*.

G2: Option A, [reluctantly]

Keep in mind that a verb can be a visible or an invisible action (like *to think*), as well as a state of being. In the sentence *I reluctantly went on holiday to sunny Spain.*, *went* (past simple tense of *go*) is the visible action, the verb.

Adverb, on the other hand, tells us *when*, *how*, or *where* the verb happens. In the sentence, *reluctantly* is the adverb. It gives more information on the *how* of the verb *went*.

G3: Option B, [*The sentence is wrong.*]

The thing that is wrong in the sentence is *your*. It should be *you're*, which is the contraction for *you are*.

G4: Option B, [*I hung the picture yesterday.*]

Hung is the past simple and past participle of *hang*. *Hanged* is also the past simple of *hang*.

However, *hanged* is normally used in the sense of a capital punishment. For example: *He was hanged for committing murder.*

G5: Option B, [*The child jumped and screamed in anger.*]

Remember: a verb can be a visible or an invisible action, as well as a state of being. In this sentence, *jumped* and *screamed* are the two verbs. They are visible actions.

G6: Option C, [*worse*]

Comparative adjectives, like *worse*, are used to

compare two things, to show the amount, number, quality or degree of difference.

Superlative adjectives, on the other hand, are used to compare three or more things.

Tip: The superlative adjective for *bad* is the *worst*.

G7: Option D, *[loveliest]*

Superlative adjectives, like *loveliest*, are used to compare three or more things, to show the amount, number, quality or degree of difference.

Comparative adjectives, on the other hand, are used to compare two things.

Tip: The comparative adjective for lovely is *lovelier*.

G8: Option B, *[better]*

Comparative adjectives, like *better*, are used to compare two things, to show the amount, number, quality or degree of difference.

Superlative adjectives, on the other hand, are used to compare three or more things.

> **Tip:** The superlative adjective for *good* is the *best*.

G9: Option C, [*loudest*]

Keep in mind that an adjective usually describes a noun. In the sentence, the noun is *kid*; therefore, the adjective is *loudest*.

Tip: Usually, adjectives go before the nouns they describe. *Loudest* is a superlative adjective.

G10: Option C, [*verb: cycled / noun: work*]

In the sentence, *work* serves a noun, while *cycled* is the main verb.

Tip: Words can perform different functions in a sentence. For example, *work* is also a verb, so is *last*, which can also function as a noun, an adverb, or an adjective.

G11: Option B, [*It's wrong.*]

In the sentence, *their* is wrong. It should be *there*. Remember that *their* is a determiner. It is used to show belonging: *They left their books.*

There is used in a sentence before the different

forms of *be (is, was, were, are)*. *There* is also used to refer to a place or position.

Here are two examples: *There were many students in the classroom. Johnson put the books there.*

G12: Option A, *[beliefs]*

Don't forget that *belief* is a noun, while *believe* is a verb.

Tip: To form the plural of *belief*, simply add s. It is different from *leaf*, which changes to *leaves* for its plural form.

G13: Option D, *[excited: adjective / child: noun]*

Remember that an adjective usually describes a noun. In the sentence, the noun is *child*; therefore, the adjective is *excited*.

Tip: Usually, adjectives go before the nouns they describe. *Excited* is also the past simple of verb to *excite*.

G14: Option A, *[me]*

Remember that although *I* and *me* are personal

pronouns, there is a difference between them. Use *I* when you are the subject of the sentence. Use *me* when you are the object of the sentence.

Remember also to put the other person first. So, you say: **you and I**, not **I and you.**

Tips: If you come before the main verb in the sentence (the subject), use *I*. If you come after the main verb in the sentence (the object), use **me.**

G15: Option C, [in]

In a sentence, a preposition is a word used to show place, position, time or movement.

Tip: There are different types of prepositions: preposition of place/position, preposition of time, preposition of movement. In the sentence in question G15, *in* is a preposition of place.

G16: Option B, [This sentence is incorrect.]

Let's look at the sentence again. *My favourite pastimes are cooking my pets and painting.*

The sentence is incorrect because it needs a comma after *cooking*. You can also add a colon after *are*. If not, you might end up cooking your pets.

Remember that correct punctuation is important for our sentences to make sense.

So, the correct sentence should look like this: *My favourite pastimes are cooking, my pets and painting.* Or *My favourite pastimes are: cooking, my pets and painting.*

G17: Option D, [*through*]

Like we mentioned above, a preposition is a word used to show place, position, time or movement.

Tip: There are different types of prepositions: preposition of place/position, preposition of time, preposition of movement.
In the sentence *The children had to trudge through the mud.*, the word *through* is a preposition of movement.

G18: Option B, [*was*]

Remember that **was** comes from the verb to **be**.

Tip: The irregular verb *be* takes different forms: *is, are, am, was, were, been, being.* The use of each form depends on whether it performs a *singular* or a *plural* function; or whether it is used in the *past* or in the *present* tense.

G19: Option C, *[The chef loves cooking.]*

Option A is wrong because the sentence doesn't begin with a capital letter.

Option B is wrong because the sentence doesn't end with a full stop.

Option D is wrong because the verb *love* doesn't agree with the singular subject: *chef*.

Tip: The subject of a sentence must agree with the verb. Therefore, singular subjects take singular verbs; plural subjects take plural verbs.

G20: Option A, *[No, it's not correct.]*

The word *sheep* doesn't have a plural form. Therefore, it's only correct to say and write *I have one sheep; Amber has 100 sheep.*

G21: Option A, *[dark / dreary]*

Remember: *antonyms* are words that are opposite in meaning to other words.

Tip: On the other hand, *synonyms* are words that are similar in meaning to other words.

G22: Option A, [*because*]

The conjunction, *because*, is used to show a reason. In the sentence, it shows the reason for liking horse-riding.

Tip: Here are other common conjunctions and their uses: *and* is used to show an added information, or to join independent clauses in a sentence; *but* is used to show contrast; *so* is used to show result.

G23: Option D, [*joyfully*]

Remember that an adverb tells us *when*, *how*, or *where* the verb happens. In the sentence, **joyfully** is the adverb. It gives more information on the *how* of the verb **skipped**.

Tip: Most adverbs end in **ly**.

G24: Option B, [*and*]

The conjunction *and* is used to show an added information, or to join independent clauses in a sentence.
In the sentence, it joins the two independent clauses into one sentence.

Tip: Here are other common conjunctions and their uses: *but* is used to show contrast; *so* is used to show result; *because* is used to show a reason.

G25: Option C, [*I think it's going to rain.*]

Keep in mind that *its* (without apostrophe) is used to show that something belongs to another thing that has been mentioned earlier in the sentence. For example: *The dog lost its tooth.*

On the other hand, *it's* (with apostrophe) is the short form (or contraction) for *it is* and *it has.*

G26: Option A, [*an adjective*]

Remember that an adjective usually describes a noun. In the sentence, the noun is *forest*; therefore, the adjective is *scary.*

Tip: Usually, adjectives go before the nouns they describe.

G27: Option B, [*You and I are friends.*]

Remember that although *I* and *me* are personal pronouns, there is a difference between them. Use *I* when you are the subject of the sentence.

Use *me* when you are the object of the sentence.

Remember also to put the other person first. So, you say and write **you and I**, not **I and you.**

Tips: If you come before the main verb in the sentence, use *I* (subject personal pronoun). If you come after the main verb in the sentence, use *me* (object personal pronoun).

G28: Option C, [*The proper noun in this sentence is Catwalk Cafe.*]

Remember that a proper noun is the name of an organization, person, place, or company.

Tip: Proper nouns are spelt with initial capital letters.

G29: Option B, [*an adverb*]

An adverb tells us *when, how,* or *where* the verb happens. In the sentence (**I happily ran through the scary forest.**), *happily* is the adverb. It gives more information on the *how* of the verb *ran.*

Tip: Most adverbs end in **ly.**

G30: Options B *[I don't want any help.]* & C *[I do not want any help.]*

Options B and C are actually the same but in Option C, *don't* is written in full *do not*.

Remember that Option A is wrong because there are two negatives (*don't/no*) in the sentence.

G31: Option B, *[it]*

Remember that *it* is a pronoun that can be used as an indefinite object in a sentence or used to refer to something that has already been mentioned.

G32: Option B, *[sunny]*

Let's bring back the sentence again. *I reluctantly went on holiday to sunny Spain.* Remember that an adjective usually describes a noun. The nouns in the sentence are *holiday* and *Spain.* But *sunny* is the adjective that describes *Spain.*

Tip: Usually, adjectives go before the nouns they describe.

G33: Option A, *[Nathanial (my best friend) came to my house yesterday.]*

Remember that brackets (also called parentheses, mainly in the US) are used to insert additional information within a sentence.

G34: Option C, [newspaper]

Remember that a noun is a name. The word *newspaper* is a common noun.

G35: Option C, [The box is ready.] and Option D, [The box of sweets is ready.]

Option A is wrong, because *box* should be *boxes* (to agree with *are*).
Option B is wrong, because of the same reason.

Tip: The subject of a sentence must agree with the verb. Therefore, singular subjects take singular verbs; plural subjects take plural verbs.

G36: Option C, [obviously]

An adverb tells us *when*, *how*, or *where* the verb happens. In the sentence, *obviously* is the adverb. It gives more information on the *how* of the verb *shouting*.

> **Tip:** Most adverbs end in *ly*.

G37: Option C, [*went / bought*]

Remember that a verb can be a visible or an invisible action, as well as a state of being. In the sentence, *went*, (past simple of *go*) and *bought* (past simple of *buy*) are the verbs. They are visible actions.

G38: Option A, [*fragile / delicate*]

An *antonym* is a word that is opposite in meaning to another word.
A *synonym* is a word that is similar in meaning to another word.

G39: Option C, [*us / We*]

The pronouns *us* and *we* are appropriate to complete the sense in the sentence.

Here is what the sentence should look like: *The dog chased us down the road. We ran because we were scared.*

Tip: The pronoun *us* is an object pronoun, while

we is a subject pronoun.

G40: Option B, [*me*]

Don't forget that although *I* and *me* are personal pronouns, there is a difference between them. Use *I* when you are the subject of the sentence. Use *me* when you are the object of the sentence.

Remember also to put the other person first. So, you say and write *you and I*, not *I and you.*

Tips: If you come before the main verb in the sentence, use *I* (subject personal pronoun). If you come after the main verb in the sentence, use *me* (object personal pronoun).

G41: Option B, [*I*]

Keep in mind that although *I* and *me* are personal pronouns, there is a difference between them. Use *I* when you are the subject of the sentence. Use *me* when you are the object of the sentence.

Remember also to put the other person first. So, you say and write *you and I*, not *I and you.*

Tips: If you come before the main verb in the sentence, use *I* (subject personal pronoun). If you come after the main verb in the sentence, use *me* (object personal pronoun).

G42: Option B, *[It was late for you and me.]*

Remember that although *I* and *me* are personal pronouns, there is a difference between them. Use *I* when you are the subject of the sentence. Use *me* when you are the object of the sentence.

Remember also to put the other person first. So, you say and write *you and I*, not *I and you*.

Tips: If you come before the main verb in the sentence, use *I* (subject personal pronoun). If you come after the main verb in the sentence, use *me* (object personal pronoun).

G43: Option A, *[noun: prophecy / verb: prophesy]*

Notice the difference in the spellings. The noun *prophecy* is spelt with a *c*, and the pronunciation is *si* (like *see*) at the end. The verb *prophesy* is spelt with an *s* and the pronunciation is *sai* (like *sir i*) at the end.

G44: Option A, *[noun: advice / verb: advise]*

Notice the difference in the spellings. The noun *advice* (spelt with *c*), means a piece of information or an opinion (usually a helpful one), that someone offers you.

On the other hand, the verb *advise* (spelt with *s*), means to give that piece of information or an opinion (usually a helpful one), to someone.

Tips: *advice* (noun) is the information or an opinion
advise (verb) is to give the information or opinion

G45: Option A, [noun: device / verb: devise]

Notice the difference in the spellings.

The noun *device* means an object or machine that has been made for a particular purpose. It can also mean a method of doing something.

The verb *devise* means to invent or to plan an object, a system, or a method.

G46: Option B, [noun: practice / verb: practise]

Notice the difference in the spellings. The noun *practice* (spelt with *c*), in British English, refers to the act or the place of doing something (not the doing itself). It also refers to the professional business of, for example, dentists, doctors, and lawyers.

On the other hand, the verb *practise* (spelt with *s*) means to do something repeatedly or regularly in order to acquire or to improve skills and knowledge.

G47: Option C, [*sun / trees / car*]

Remember that a noun is a name. The words *sun/trees/car* are common nouns (common names).

G48: Option A, [*over*]

Remember that in a sentence, a preposition is a word used to show place, position, time or movement.

Tip: There are different types of prepositions: preposition of place/position, preposition of time, preposition of movement.

In the sentence (*The hurdler jumped over the hurdles.*), the word *over* is a preposition of movement.

G49: Option A, [a verb]

Remember that the action (the doing) in the sentence is the verb.

Tip: A verb can be a visible or an invisible action, as well as a state of being. In this sentence, *helped* is the verb. It is a visible action.

G50: Option A, [Was you at the party?]

Remember that *was* and *were* come from the verb to *be*.

1. Even though *you* can be singular or plural, it is always used with a plural verb, hence *you are* (present tense), *you were* (past tense).

To form questions, swap the words, to become *Are you...? Were you...?* Therefore, it's incorrect to say or write *Was you...?*

2. The irregular verb *be* takes different forms: *is, are, am, was, were, been, being.* The use of each form depends on whether it performs a *singular* or a *plural* function, or whether it is used in the *past* or in the *present* tense.

G51: Option C, [*an adjective*]

Remember that an adjective usually describes a noun. Although the nouns in the sentence are *girl* and *swing*, *chatty* is the adjective that describes the *girl*.

Tip: Usually, adjectives go before the nouns they describe.

G52: Option D, [*a verb*]

Remember that the action (the doing) in the sentence is the verb.

Tip: A verb can be a visible or an invisible action, as well as a state of being. In this sentence, *play* is the verb. It is a visible action.

Verbs in the infinitive (unchanged form) are usually preceded by *to* (*to eat, to play, to run*).

G53: Option C, [*leaves*]

Remember that *leaf* is one of those nouns that have irregular plurals.

Tip: Other common nouns with irregular plurals

are *loaf – loaves, sheep – sheep, mouse – mice, knife – knives.*

G54: Option A, [*a noun*]

In the sentence (*I helped the chatty girl to play on the* **swing***.*), *swing* is a noun.

Tip: The word *swing* is also a verb, which can be used to show a back and forth movement.

G55: Option B, [*theirs*]

Remember that *theirs* is a possessive pronoun which is used to show that something belongs to some people.

Tip: It is incorrect to write *their's.*

G56. Option B, [*knives*]

Remember that *knife* is one of those nouns that have irregular plurals.

Tip: Other common nouns with irregular plurals are *loaf – loaves, sheep – sheep, mouse – mice, leaf – leaves.*

G57: Option A, [*Samuel packed his bag and ran to school.*]

Remember that the action (the doing) in the sentence is the verb.

Tip: A verb can be a visible or an invisible action, as well as a state of being.

In the sentence (*Samuel packed his bag and ran to school.*), *packed* and *ran* are the verbs. Both are visible actions.

G58: Option C, [*quickly / silently*]

An adverb tells us *when*, *how*, or *where* the verb happens.

In the sentence (*The mouse scuttled quickly and silently across the floor.*), *quickly* and *silently* are the adverbs.

Both give more information on the *how* of the verb *scuttled*. **Tip:** Most adverbs end in *ly*.

G59: Option B, [*noun: altar / verb: alter*]

These two words have a similar pronunciation. But

take note of the difference in their spellings.

Get it right
The noun *altar* (spelt with *a*) is the name of a type of table (or something similar) that is used in a Christian church or in other religions or religious ceremonies.

The verb *alter* (spelt with *e*) means to change something or to make something to be different.

G60: Option B, *[hers]*

Remember that *hers* (without apostrophe) is a possessive pronoun which is used to show that something belongs to someone, usually a female. **Tip:** It is incorrect to write *her's*.

G61: Option B, *[complex sentence]*

A complex sentence has at least one independent clause (the main clause), and at least one dependent or subordinate clause (the minor clause).

The dependent clause cannot stand as a separate sentence, but the independent clause can stand as a separate sentence.

Let's bring up the sentence again. *After my friend left, I started doing my homework at 2 o'clock.*

The first part of the sentence, *After my friend left,* is the dependent or minor clause. It doesn't really make sense on its own.

However, the second part, *I started doing my homework at 2 o'clock,* is the independent or the main clause. On its own, it makes sense.

G62: Option A, [*The sentence is incorrect.*]

The sentence (*This is my instruments.*) is incorrect because the determiners *this* and *these* have different functions: *this* is used in the singular sense (*this student...*); *these* is used in the plural sense (*these students...*).

Therefore, the correct sentence should be *These are my instruments.* Or *This is my instrument.* **Tip:** *this* – singular / *these* – plural.

G63: Option A, [*Yes, something is wrong.*]

The sentence is wrong because of the small letter *i*. Remember that *I* must always be in capital letter, anytime you use it to refer to yourself.

G64: Option C, [*complex sentence*]

A complex sentence has at least one independent clause (the main clause), and one dependent or subordinate clause (the minor clause).

The dependent clause cannot stand as a separate sentence, but the independent clause can stand as a separate sentence.

Let's bring up the sentence again. *Despite the bad weather, the fair raised a lot of money for the charity.*

The first part of the sentence, *Despite the bad weather*, is the dependent or minor clause. It doesn't really make sense on its own.

However, the second part, *the fair raised a lot of money for the charity*, is the independent or main clause. On its own, it makes sense.

G65: Option B, [*No*]

The sentence is incorrect because the subject, *everybody*, does not agree with the verb *are*.

Note that *everybody* is a singular pronoun, while *are* is a plural verb. They don't go together. The correct answer is *Everybody in the college is finishing today.*

Tip: The subject of a sentence must agree with the verb. Therefore, singular subjects go with singular verbs; plural subjects go with plural verbs.

G66: Option A, *[a noun]*

Remember that a noun is a name. However, the word *book* is a noun and a verb. In this sentence (*The library assistant told Joe to return the **book** he borrowed.*), *book* is a noun.

G67: Option B, *[a verb]*

Notice the difference in the use of *book* in questions G66 and G67. While *book* is a noun in question G66, it is a verb (to *book*) in question G67.

Tip: Verbs in the infinitive (unchanged) form are usually preceded by *to (to book, to eat, to play, to run).*

G68: Option A, *[unattractive / unsightly]*

An *antonym* is a word that is opposite in meaning

to another word.

A *synonym* is a word that is similar in meaning to another word.

G69: Option B, [No]

The sentence is incorrect because the subject, *everything*, does not agree with the verb *have*.

Note that *everything* is a singular pronoun, while *have* is a plural verb. They don't go together. The correct answer is *Everything has been done.*

Tip: The subject of a sentence must agree with the verb. Therefore, singular subjects go with singular verbs; plural subjects go with plural verbs.

G70: Option C, [Paul didn't want no more food.]

Remember that Option C is wrong because there are two negatives (*didn't/no*) in the sentence.

G71: Option A, [the two drivers shook hands]

Remember that a complex sentence has at least one independent clause (the main clause), and one dependent or subordinate clause (the minor clause).

The dependent clause cannot stand as a separate sentence, but the independent clause can stand as a separate sentence.

Here is that sentence again: *After the race had finished, the two drivers shook hands.*

The first part of the sentence, *After the race had finished,* is the dependent or minor clause. It doesn't really make sense on its own.

However, the second part, *the two drivers shook hands,* is the independent or main clause. On its own, it makes sense.

Tip: On the other hand, a compound sentence has two or more main clauses. These clauses are then joined, using conjunctions. Look at this example: *Stephen won the best swimmer award and Priti won the beauty contest.*). In this sentence, there are two main (or independent) clauses, joined using a coordinating conjunction *and.*

G72: Option A, [*Although they were tired*]

Remember that a complex sentence has at least one independent clause (the main clause), and one dependent or subordinate clause (the minor clause).

The dependent clause cannot stand as a separate sentence, but the independent clause can stand as a separate sentence.

Let's bring the sentence back. *Although they were tired, the children kept running.*

The first part of the sentence, *Although they were tired*, is the dependent or minor clause. It doesn't really make sense on its own.

However, the second part, *the children continued running*, is the independent or main clause. On its own, it makes sense.

On the other hand, a compound sentence has two or more main clauses. These clauses are then joined, using a coordinating conjunction.

Look at this example: *Stephen won the best swimmer award and Priti won the beauty contest.* In this sentence, there are two main (or independent) clauses, joined using a coordinating conjunction *and*.

G73: Option B, *[tomorrow]*

Remember that an adverb tells us *when*, *how*, or *where* the verb happens. In the sentence, (*I'll go swimming tomorrow.*), the adverb is *tomorrow*. It gives more information on the *when* of the verb to *go*.

Tip: Most adverbs end in **ly**.

G74: Option B, *[haven't they?]*

Don't forget that a tag question is usually added at the end of a sentence, as part of the sentence. It prompts the listener to respond.

A sentence with a tag question has two parts: the first part is the statement while the following part is the tag question. A comma separates both parts.

If the statement is negative, the tag question should be positive. But if the statement is positive, then the tag question should be negative.

For example: *They've been here before, haven't they?* In this example, the first part of the sentence (the statement) is positive, therefore, the second part (the tag question) should be negative.

If the statement part of the question has any form of *be, do, have*, the tag question should include that.

For example: *It was cold last night, wasn't it?* In this example, the first part of the sentence (the statement) includes *was*, therefore, the second part of the sentence (the tag question) should include *was*, but in the negative (*wasn't*).

G75: Option B, [*Millie*]

Remember that the subject of a sentence is the giver of the action of the main verb in the sentence. In this case, *Millie* is the subject because *Millie* performs the action of *played*, which is the main verb in the sentence.

G76: Option C, [*cat*]

Remember that the object of a sentence receives the action of the main verb in the sentence. In this case, the *cat* receives the action of *stroked*, which is the main verb in the sentence.

G77: Sentence A, [*My favourite superheroes are Batman and Superman*]

Here, the correctly spelt plural is *superheroes*. In sentence B, *thiefs* is wrong. The plural form is *thieves*. In sentence C, *berrys* is wrong. It should be *berries*. In sentence D, *boy's* is wrong. The correct plural form is *boys*.

G78: Option B, [*compound sentence*]

A compound sentence has two or more main clauses. These clauses are then joined, using a coordinating conjunction.

The sentence in question G78 (*The Alsatian came out last night and its barking filled the air.*), is a good example of a compound sentence. It has two main (or independent) clauses, joined using a coordinating conjunction *and*.

G79: Option C [*do you?*]

Don't forget that a tag question is usually added at the end of a sentence, as part of the sentence. It prompts the listener to respond.

A sentence with a tag question has two parts: the first part is the statement while the following part is the tag question. A comma separates both parts.

If the statement is negative, the tag question should be positive. But if the statement is positive, then the tag question should be negative.

For example: *They've been here before, haven't they?* In this example, the first part of the sentence (the statement) is positive, therefore, the second part (the tag question) should be negative.

If the statement part of the question has any form of *be, do, have,* the tag question should include that.

For example: *It was cold last night, wasn't it?* In this example, the first part of the sentence (the statement) includes *was,* therefore the second part of the sentence (the tag question) should include *was,* but in the negative (*wasn't*).

G80: Option B [have we?]

Don't forget that a tag question is usually added at the end of a sentence, as part of the sentence. It prompts the listener to respond. A sentence with a tag question has two parts: the first part is the statement while the following part is the tag question. A comma separates both parts.

If the statement is negative, the tag question should be positive. But if the statement is positive, then the tag question should be negative.

For example: *They've been here before, haven't they?* In this example, the first part of the sentence (the statement) is positive, therefore, the second part (the tag question) should be negative.

If the statement part of the question has any form of *be, do, or have*, the tag question should include that.

For example: *It was cold last night, wasn't it?* In this example, the first part of the sentence (the statement) includes *was*, therefore the second part of the sentence (the tag question should include *was*, but in the negative (*wasn't*).

G81: Option B [true]

Articles are of two major types: definite article and indefinite articles. Definite article is *the*. Indefinite articles are *a* or *an*.

We always use the definite article *the* before a noun, to refer to a specific person, issue, time period, currencies, or place. The indefinite articles (*a* and *an*) are used to refer to things (nouns) in a non-specific way.

The indefinite article *a* is used with words that begin with consonants (for example: *a car*), while indefinite article *an* is used with words that begin with a vowel.

The definite article *the* is used with many other things, including before:

- superlatives (for example: *the* greatest, *the* best, *the* most beautiful)
- some names of countries and institutions: (for example: *the* UK, *the* USA, *the* United Nations)
- specific things (for example: *the* British Empire)

Tips

- Indefinite article *a* is used with words like *uniform* (*a uniform*) and *university* (*a university*) because they don't make the same vowel sound like *umbrella* which uses *an* (*an umbrella*).
- Words beginning with a silent *h* (like *hour*) also use *an* (*an hour*).
- English language vowels include the alphabets *a, e, i, o, u*.
- English language consonants include the rest of the alphabets.

G82: Option A [*true*]

Articles are of two major types: definite article and indefinite articles. Definite article is *the*. Indefinite articles are *a* or *an*.

We always use the definite article *the* before a noun, to refer to a specific person, issue, time period, currencies, or place. The indefinite articles (*a* and *an*) are used to refer to things (nouns) in a non-specific way.

The indefinite article *a* is used with words that begin with consonants (for example: a car), while indefinite article *an* is used with words that begin with a vowel.

The definite article *the* is used with many other things, including before:
- superlatives (for example: *the* greatest, *the* best, *the* most beautiful)
- some names of countries and institutions: (for example: *the* UK, *the* USA, *the* United Nations)
- specific things (for example: *the* British Empire)

Tips
- Indefinite article *a* is used with words like *uniform* (*a uniform*) and *university* (*a university*) because they don't make the same vowel sound like *umbrella* which uses *an* (*an umbrella*).
- Words beginning with a silent *h* (like *hour*) also use *an* (*an hour*).

- English language vowels include the alphabets *a, e, i, o, u.*
- English language consonants include the rest of the alphabets.

IRREGULAR VERBS

VERB	PAST SIMPLE	PAST PARTICIPLE
Awake	Awoke	Awoken
Be	Was, Were	Been
Beat	Beat	Beaten
Become	Became	Become
Begin	Began	Begun
Bend	Bent	Bent
Bet	Bet	Bet
Bid	Bid	Bid
Bite	Bit	Bitten

Blow	Blew	Blown
Break	Broke	Broken
Bring	Brought	Brought
Broadcast	Broadcast	Broadcast
Build	Built	Built
Burn	Burned/Burnt	Burned/Burnt
Buy	Bought	Bought
Catch	Caught	Caught
Choose	Chose	Chosen
Come	Came	Come
Cost	Cost	Cost
Cut	Cut	Cut
Dig	Dug	Dug
Do	Did	Done
Draw	Drew	Drawn
Dream	Dreamed or Dreamt	Dreamed or Dreamt

Drive	Drove	Driven
Drink	Drank	Drunk
Eat	Ate	Eaten
Fall	Fell	Fallen
Feel	Felt	Felt
Fight	Fought	Fought
Find	Found	Found
Fly	Flew	Flown
Forget	Forgot	Forgotten
Forgive	Forgave	Forgiven
Freeze	Froze	Frozen
Get	Got	Got/Gotten
Give	Gave	Given
Go	Went	Gone
Grow	Grew	Grown
Hang	Hung	Hung

Have	Had	Had
Hear	Heard	Heard
Hide	Hid	Hidden
Hit	Hit	Hit
Hold	Held	Held
Hurt	Hurt	Hurt
Keep	Kept	Kept
Know	Knew	Known
Lay	Laid	Laid
Lead	Led	Led
Learn	Learned/Learnt	Learned/Learnt
Leave	Left	Left
Lend	Lent	Lent
Let	Let	Let
Lie	Lay	Lain
Lose	Lost	Lost

Make	Made	Made
Mean	Meant	Meant
Meet	Met	Met
Pay	Paid	Paid
Put	Put	Put
Read	Read	Read
Ride	Rode	Ridden
Ring	Rang	Rung
Rise	Rose	Risen
Run	Ran	Run
Say	Said	Said
See	Saw	Seen
Sell	Sold	Sold
Send	Sent	Sent
Show	Showed	Showed/Shown
Shut	Shut	Shut

Sing	Sang	Sung
Sink	Sank	Sunk
Sit	Sat	Sat
Sleep	Slept	Slept
Speak	Spoke	Spoken
Spend	Spent	Spent
Stand	Stood	Stood
Stink	Stank	Stunk
Swim	Swam	Swum
Take	Took	Taken
Teach	Taught	Taught
Tear	Tore	Torn
Tell	Told	Told
Think	Thought	Thought
Throw	Threw	Thrown
Understand	Understood	Understood

Wake	Woke	Woken
Wear	Wore	Worn
Win	Won	Won
Write	Wrote	Written

THE AUTHOR

Obinna was an assistant editor at NewsAfrica magazine, a pan-African newsmagazine based in London.

Until recently, he was an English language lecturer in a further education college in the UK. He now writes, and teaches English language privately, having taught the subject for over eight years.

Basildon, England
February 2020